Performance Reviews Suck

"I have a great idea that will revitalize the company, prevent bankruptcy and save hundreds of jobs. But I'm saving it for the day before my performance review."

Copyright 2015 Keith Lee

All rights reserved. Small sections of this book are intended for you to use in your business to improve your customer service. You may reproduce those sections for use in your business. With the exception of the above, this book may not be reproduced in whole or in part by any means without the permission of the publisher.

For more information, contact Keith Lee, 14248 SE 270th Place, Kent, WA 98032.

Discounts are available for bulk purchases.

Email Keith@KeithLee.com

Just listen to what they're called - **Performance Review**, or **Personal Development Interview.** If you're on the receiving end, which would you prefer, being reviewed in hindsight, or being developed?

What if you're the manager? Which would you rather do, review someone in hind-sight or develop them?

Which would be more rewarding, and **get better results?**

Contents

Author's Introduction
   They All Laughed When I Told Them I
   Don't Have Employee Headaches 7

Chapter 1
   Performance Reviews Suck 13

Chapter 2
   Your Employees Can't Be Scarier
   Than a Teenager 17

Chapter 3
   Catch People Doing Things Right 23

Chapter 4
   You Must Manage the 95-Percentors 29

Chapter 5
   You Must Have an Effective Feedback System 33

Chapter 6
   7 Components of an Effective
   Performance Management System 41

Chapter 7
   Situational Leadership –
   Just Another "Feel Good" Buzzword? 53

Chapter 8
　　The Personal Development Interview...
　　The Powering Force of an Effective Performance
　　Management System the Power of Systems 59

Chapter 9
　　Putting It All Together 77

Author's Introduction

They All Laughed When I Told Them I Don't Have Employee Problems...

"When petty squabbles break out in the office, call Sharon. She used to run a daycare center."

Believe me I know what it's like. I've been there, with you, in that same conversation... Whenever you get together with other business owners the conversation always gets around to the headaches — trying to get your employees functioning as an effective team and functioning at a high level as individuals and, in general, getting things done consistently right by system, rather than by fighting fires and fixing mistakes.

In fact, not to long ago I was in one of those little get-togethers and someone asked me about my employee problems. When I said, "I don't have employee problems" they all laughed. They thought I was being sarcastic.

But then afterwards a couple of them asked me if I was serious - if I really don't have employee headaches. They asked me for the secret. I told them, it's really not a secret, it's the systems we have in place. They literally begged me – guilted me – into writing this book.

You've probably been at this long enough to know that you don't have all of the answers, and you likely have enough employees that you know the answer certainly isn't MORE employees.

Things just don't seem to change - But they can...

What would it mean to you if you could get all of your employees functioning as an effective team and functioning at a high level as individuals and, in general, getting things done consistently right by system, rather than by fighting fires and fixing mistakes?

If you know you could achieve more, build the business you've always wanted, take that vacation and actually forget about work, and have a less stressful, and more enjoyable home life, if only everybody else around you could be counted on more, this will be life-changing for you.

THIS IS ABOUT CONTROL & FREEDOM

Isn't that why you became a business owner in the first place? Of course it is. But...

I know, I was there. As an owner of a wholesale distribution business that grew from one employee to more than sixty, I know all too well that far too often the business seems to control you rather than you controlling it.

And freedom?... That's what I wanted, but I was never ever really free. **IT was always there** - The Business - the problems, the headaches, the employees, wondering what I'm going to need to "deal with" next.

The business that was supposed to set me free had done the opposite.

Why is that? Why does every business owner have the same problems?

Too many hours, too many problems - too often working on mundane, menial tasks rather than on the important. The things that lead to real growth, more profits, and the business you've always wanted.

What if you could get everyone working together, going in the same direction and taking responsibility? What if you didn't have to take care of all of those problems? What if you had time to spend on the really important? What if you didn't have to spend time on mundane, menial, everyday tasks and could work on the important? When you can do that you'll not only have a better, more profitable business; but you'll have a less stressful, more productive life outside of work.

As I mentioned, I own a wholesale distribution company. We've been in business since 1970. I became the owner in the 80's, and by the 90's I was right there with my business owner friends bitching and moaning about employees. But that all changed when I learned how to truly develop people and get the best out of them.

In this book you'll discover how to implement a performance feedback system that you'll love, your employees will love, and that most importantly; gets the performance you want.

Would You Dare?

I own a wholesale distribution business. In the last 12 months we delivered 46,432 orders to 8,645 clients. Every one of those clients gets this message from me many times throughout the year, "If we ever let you down please call 800-426-5708 right away so we can make it right, if you're still not happy call me on my direct line at 253-859-7310 so I can make it right."

Would you dare do that?

Here's the kicker - I'm lonely... like the Old Maytag Repairman. I only get about one call every other month from a client we've let down.

CHAPTER 1

Performance Reviews Suck!

"I like to begin every performance review with a compliment. Boy, I look good today!"

This book should have been titled *Performance Management, How to Get the Best out of Every Team Member.* I didn't title it that because most people think that the only type of performance management is performance reviews and everyone knows that **performance reviews suck.**

Shortly after developing my Performance Management System we had a friend over for dinner. My wife told her that I had been in Florida and Michigan giving presentations on my system, so she said, "Tell me about this management stuff you're doing."

She was retired from a large aerospace company in the Puget Sound area that I knew did performance reviews so I asked, "When you were at B***** you had performance reviews, right?"

She rolled her eyes and said, "Yes."

I asked, "What did you think of them?"

She replied, "They Sucked!"

You need to understand that Mary is one of those people who wouldn't say sh** if she had a mouthful, so I knew I had the title for my book, **Performance Reviews Suck.**

Chapter 2

Your Employees Can't Be Scarier Than a Teenager

"Some men are born great, some men achieve greatness, and some men have teenagers at home so they don't mind spending 18 hours a day at the office."

I speak to a lot of groups and I often ask, "How many of you have been on the giving or receiving end of a performance review?" Most of the people in the room raise their hand. I then ask, "How many of you like performance reviews, think they are motivating, and that they lead to the results that the organization wants?" Once in a while, a hand or two will go up, but most often, no one raises their hand.

Going back to my conversation with Mary, I told her a little about PDIs and then asked, "Just listen to what they're called - Performance Review, or Personal Development Interview. If you're on the receiving end, which would you prefer, being reviewed in hind sight, or being developed?"

Her reply: "Being developed, of course."

I then asked, "What if you're the manager? Which would you rather do, review someone in hind sight or develop them? Which would be more rewarding, and get better results?"

Her answer again, "Being developed."

If you've ever been on the giving or receiving end of a performance review you know they suck. Everyone hates them. They're de-motivating, discouraging and most importantly... they don't lead to the behavior you want.

Performance Reviews are like trying to drive your car by looking in the rearview mirror.

Performance Reviews are like trying to drive your car by looking in the rearview mirror.

As a parent of a teenager, can you imagine getting the performance you want from your kid by having an annual performance review? Would every six months work? How about quarterly? Your employees can not be scarier than a teenager.

Your employees can't be scarier than a teenager!

In 1993 I created my Management System that sets expectations for exactly what needed to be done, but in regards to Performance Management we were still doing Performance Reviews. While trying to put on my "best face" for our team in regards to performance reviews, the truth is I hated them. I knew they were de-motivating, and finally determined that they were actually doing more harm than good and stopped doing them.

I met Vince Zirpoli in 2005 and knew immediately that I found the missing link. My management system was now complete with a Performance Management System that actually worked.

CHAPTER 3

Catch People Doing Things Right

"Sometimes I like to walk past your desk without criticizing you. Just to see that funny, confused look on your face."

In this chapter we'll discuss how to replace demotivating, discouraging and counterproductive performance reviews with motivating, inspiring, and most importantly, PRODUCTIVE Personal Development Interviews.

When employed properly, an effective performance management system permeates the organization with a philosophy of catching people doing things right. Most businesses focus on catching people doing things wrong.

Catching people doing things wrong is called management by exception. When businesses utilize management by exception, they're watching for people to do things incorrectly. As a result, they stymie creativity in the organization. If every time I do something wrong the boss catches me, but he doesn't catch me when I'm doing things right, then I fail to step up really help the organization grow by using my creativity.

Conversely, when we start catching people doing things right, we encourage empowerment. People start to do things in the organization. Productivity improves on an ongoing basis. Because of this the improvement in the organization doesn't just come from management, but employees and management are interacting with each other. People are picking each other up. The organization is permeated with a motivating environment.

The second benefit that comes as a result of an effective performance management system is that you create a learning organization. People want to work in a place where they can grow, where they can enjoy themselves, where they can use their creativity to help the organization grow, and that happens in a learning organization.

In addition, in a learning organization, you have lots of help finding things that are broken and fixing them. You also have the people who are closest to the job, closest to co-workers and suppliers, and closest to your customers looking for ways to improve.

Before we discuss Personal Development Interviews in depth, it's important to understand a couple of other concepts. The first is that in all organizations, systems have at a minimum influence, and at maximum control over the behavior of individuals. It's critical to understand this because if you don't, you'll take a Band-Aid approach to correcting situations rather than finding what system is controlling the behavior and then changing it.

The problem with this is that far too often the "systems" are not really the best way to do things, but have simply been handed down from one person to the next. Have you ever played "The Whisper Game?"

One person starts by whispering a secret at one end of the group, and the secret is whispered from person to person until it goes around the entire group. It's amazing how the original message has changed by the time it gets all the way around. Now imagine if that message was the wrong message in the first place. In other words, on the job, that particular duty was not done correctly in the first place.

Chapter 4

You Must Manage The 95-Percentors

"Who did we put in charge of writing the new mission statement?"

The second concept is the 5-percentor. If you look at any organization, you'll find about 5% of the people are self-starters. They are self-motivated. They join the organization and management says "Go in that direction," and they go in that direction. They plan, they organize, they motivate themselves, they control their activities, and they go in that direction. They do a super job.

The 5-percentor is often selected to move into management. **You are likely a 5-percentor.**

When 5-percentors move into management they're told they have to coach, motivate, train and develop people; and their automatic response is... "No one had to watch me. No one had to tell me how to do it. I just did it."

They don't understand that they are managing 95-percentors. The 95-percentors are good people, but they need coaching, leadership, development, and follow-through. The key is that the manager has to understand this, and understand that he is more than a manager, or a director. The manager needs to be a trainer, coach, facilitator, developer, motivator, counselor, and administrator.

With that said, it's critical to understand that all development is self-development. You cannot develop another person. You cannot motivate another person.

You can create an environment in which they motivate themselves. You can facilitate their development, and as you facilitate their development you have to know that you cannot be the know-it-all guru. Managers who believe they have to be the know-it-all guru do not develop people.

You want your team to use their creativity. You want to empower them. You want them to come up with ideas. You teach them the process that leads to the objectives you want. Once they've proved to you that they can get the results, it's time to turn the process over to them.

You may be like a lot of business owners who were 5-percentors. Because of your work ethic and knowledge, you became dissatisfied working for someone else and decided to start your own business.

Many business owners are very successful entrepreneurs until the management systems they learned at their old job catch up to them and creates similar frustrations in their own business… **But now, it all comes down on you.**

Chapter 5

You Must Have an Effective Feedback System

"Twenty-two years at the same job and my boss still doesn't know my name. I'm a very lucky man."

Each person needs to have **goals/objectives**. There have to be **strategies and tactics** that are employed to bring those goals and objectives to fruition. The manager has to receive **continuous feedback** letting him know what kind of progress is being made. And, there has to be an **adjustment** when you see the individual is not making progress - adjustment and corrective action that gets the individual back on target.

It's a complete system. You use this type of system every day. When you drive to a morning meeting you use this system. You set a goal of getting to the meeting on time. You develop strategies and tactics. You get to bed on time. You set your alarm to be ready to leave by a certain time. You determined the route. You get feedback from your speedometer, your odometer, and your watch. If you think you're going to be late, you step on the accelerator to get back on target. That is an effective performance feedback system, and we all utilize it every day. When we don't employ it completely, we do not have an effective system, and then we're subject to the environment as to whether we achieve our goals.

Every member of your team needs to have goals, with effective feedback, and there has to be an adjustment and corrective action taken along the way.

Think of it this way. Let's assume that you are driving an automobile, and that you want to be 50 miles down the road in one hour. It's important that you be there at a specific time, and you cannot go above the 55 mile an hour speed limit. There are no other detriments. All you have to do is drive. Your automobile is mechanically sound. You get in the automobile, and you start to drive. You can do that. It's easy right? All you have to do is average between 50 and 55 miles an hour and you'll be there on time.

Now let's assume that before you start the trip someone gets in the automobile, takes out the speedometer, the odometer, and you don't have a watch. They remove the radio, and take down all the signs along the way. They've taken away your feedback system. Now how do you feel? Do you feel the anxiety and frustration? Can you understand the frustration your team feels when you say, "Go get those goals," but with no supporting system in place to make sure they're getting the feedback and taking the necessary corrective action to get there? In order to be effective, every team member has to have individual objectives with effective continuous feedback.

Here's how most businesses develop. The entrepreneur, who is of course a 5-percentor, becomes unhappy working for a big organization. So he starts his own businesses, and he works all kinds of hours. Time means nothing to him. He wants to succeed. If he could work 50 hours a day, he would work 50 hours a day to bring his goal to fruition.

Initially, he surrounds himself with like-minded people. People who buy into his vision, who agree they can make something out of this company, and who work very hard. After a period of time, without realizing it, they start to put on the 95-percentors.

Managers often say, "I'm going to only hire 5-percentors." But, regardless of how you test, you can't tell who is a 5-percentor when you interview him. The testing only tells you their aptitude. It doesn't tell you whether they're going to do it. It tells you whether they have the ability to do it.

The owner doesn't realize that he's putting on 95-percentors because if I sit down with anyone and ask, "Tell me about yourself" - what do you think they are going to tell you? They're going to say, "Hey, man, I can do a good job. I really get out there. I work hard. I solve problems." They are going to tell you everything you want to hear. They know how to sell you, and they are going to sell you on themselves. The entrepreneur doesn't realize it and he continues to put on the 95-percentors and problems mount.

Again, the 95-percentors are good people, but they need management. They need coaching. They need help.

The business owner begins to see
- Shrinking margins
- Plateauing or falling sales
- High turnover
- Poor morale
- Poor quality or high error rate
- Declining market share
- Resistance to change
- Self Burnout

What does the entrepreneur do when he sees these problems? Initially he puts a Band-Aid approach on it. Morale's low. Let's have a party. So we have a party. Everybody's happy. Have a few drinks. And it may alleviate the problem for a short period of time, but not long after that the problems are back again.

Or let's give everybody a raise or a bonus, which does help for a short period of time, but the problem comes back because the problem that you see is not the actual problem. It's a symptom of an ineffective performance management system. These are symptoms from problems and not the real problems because if an effective performance management system is in place, these problems are minimized or eliminated. But, by addressing the symptoms, they only postpone the inevitable.

So, the entrepreneur has 1 of 4 choices:
1. If margins shrink too much, he goes out of business. If you're not making money, there's no point in staying in business.
2. In lots of organizations, the manager loves the business, and he shrinks it. It becomes a small business where they all work a hundred hours a week. He works very hard, but he has complete control. It's a centralized organization where the owner is wearing many hats. He's the marketer. He's the accountant. He does a number of things. But he stays in business.
3. Lots of managers don't want to make the change. They don't want to have to do what they have to do to change their organization and to functionalize it to become a growing organization. So they sell it to a larger company.
4. He changes his system of management. The system of management with centralized control is no longer applicable. People have to be empowered. Dele-

gation has to take place within the organization, and he or she has to take a systemic approach to it. There has to be a system in place that challenges everyone, develops everyone, and focuses on the goals that you are trying to achieve in the leadership of the company.

Chapter 6

7 Components of an Effective Performance Management System

An Effective Performance Management System has 7 components and if you understand these components and employ them, you can't fail:

1. Personal Development Interview
2. Objectives
3. Objective Focused Activities
4. Feedback
5. Measurement
6. Reinforcement
7. Coaching

1. Personal Development Interview

The Personal Development Interview (PDI) is the power source of an Effective Performance Management System. PDI's need to be regularly scheduled and held weekly, every other week, or at the very least, monthly.

In areas where you want to see a lot of change, a lot of improvement, have a lot of opportunity, or have challenges; you'll have them more often. In areas that are very much under control you'll have them less often. Typically, the lower the job function, the shorter the meeting and the less frequent.

Initially, don't expect to be an expert at PDIs. You have to work at it on a continuous basis. So often people expect change to happen overnight - it doesn't.

We change in tiny increments, and that's one of the purposes of the Personal Development Interview.

The PDI is where you'll catch people doing things right. Your job is to pick them up, keep them excited about their job, and discuss corrective action. When you're discussing corrective action it's critical that you frame it properly. When you frame it properly and sandwich the corrective action between positive reinforcement and catching them doing other things right, you'll see improvement that you never dreamed possible.

But how much time does all this take?

When I talk with business owners about Personal Development Interviews, the first question is, "Who has the time for that?"

Here are the facts: I own five businesses and conduct PDI's with the six people who report directly to me. I meet with each person, every other week, for about 20 minutes. So, on average, I spend one hour a week in PDIs. That means, because of the systems we have in place, I spend one hour per week managing five businesses. I spend the rest of my time working on the important things that grow my businesses, and the things I (enjoy) want to work on.

Research has shown that the average manager interacts with subordinates at least 37 times per week. Two, three, five minutes at a time. What if you and your subordinates got into the habit of discussing only critical issues right away and left the others for your regularly scheduled PDI? You will find that PDI's actually free up time for you, your managers, and your entire team.

Personal Development Interviews

As I mentioned before, you don't want to be the know-it-all guru during PDI's. No doubt, there are times when you have to be the know-it-all. For instance, when you're working with a brand new person, and they don't know the processes. But, shortly after that, it turns into a meeting in which you're eliciting ideas from them. You're priming the pump to help them. Each week, when they realize that you're giving their ideas consideration they'll get better at it.

When the interview is running properly, the interviewer (you or your managers) will be talking about 20% of the time and the subordinate will be talking 80% or more. Sometimes the manager only talks 5%, but these managers know what questions to ask, and they're guiding the individual. They're facilitating growth.

Let's assume you, or a manager, are having a PDI and the subordinate comes up with an idea you don't like. You need to "frame" your response. If your response is, "That won't work" they're going to close their mind. What if you responded with, "Well, you know, that could possibly work, but what will you do if...", and then introduce the reason why you know it won't work.

Maybe they have thought about your objection and found a way around it. Now two people have grown. If they haven't found a way around it, they'll come back with, "Yeah, I hadn't thought of that." Now it's time for the manager to ask, "How do you think you'll solve that problem?" The responsibility for finding solutions lies with the interviewee, not the interviewer. This is the way people grow in the organization, and you don't have to be the all-knowing King Solomon who fixes everything.

Another key to effective PDI's is that the person being interviewed should leave pumped up, ready to go after every interview. Your job, as the interviewer, is to make sure they are pumped up, ready to go, and achieve their objectives. The only time they should leave a Personal Development Interview disappointed is when you're ready to fire them.

I need to tell you I didn't believe that at first. I couldn't understand how you could get the behavior you want without constructive criticism, but when I practiced what I learned from Vince I was blown away. The reality is, if you can send them out of that meeting feeling good about themselves - not falsely, but because they achieved something, then they learned something new and made progress toward their goals. This means you're moving in the right direction.

2. Objectives

Everyone in the organization must have objectives - specific objectives - and those objectives have to relate to where you're going as an organization. If they don't relate, either directly or indirectly to where we're going as an organization, then you have to question, "Do we need that position?" If they relate to where you're going, then you're going to make progress. But you cannot manage objectives. You can only measure objective focused activities. This is critical so I'll repeat it:

**You cannot manage objectives.
You can only measure <u>objective focused activities</u>.**

3. Objective Focused Activities – The Missing Link

You **can** manage the activity in which someone engages. When they say they're going to finish a project according to schedule, that's an activity. At the end of the first week, you want to know where they are on that. How are they doing? Are they on schedule? You can't wait until the project is supposed to be completed, and find out. Again, this is like driving your car by looking through the rearview mirror. It's too late.

With a sales rep you can't manage sales, but you can manage activities that lead to sales – number of sales presentations, number of phone calls, number of letters, etc.

4. Feedback

Without adequate feedback, you're managing by circumstance. You're putting out fires. You're not managing by design. When you're getting feedback, you're reading it and taking the necessary corrective action.

This is very much like that trip you want to take 50 miles down the road, but you don't have a speedometer and just hope you get there on time and don't get a ticket. You'd never consider that.

Think of how many times you look down at the speedometer and take corrective action, maybe 2 or 3 times each mile. What's so different about the organization? You need timely feedback in order to coach, facilitate, and lead people.

You and your managers give and get feedback on Objective Focused Activities during your Personal Development Interviews.

5. Measurement

When you look at the statistics, trends, and measurable deficiencies, you're in a position to take corrective action, not based on subjective thoughts, but on actual facts that you can share with the individual. When they see the objectivity of it, they accept it.

You can't just measure the end result. You need to measure the activities leading to that end result also. You need to measure and identify strengths and weaknesses. You can then find out where problems are and address them.

As managers we must set the priorities. People respond to the areas where their supervisors show concern, but that concern has to be continuous. It can't be sporadic. You can't sit down and say, "You're doing a terrible job in this area here," and then talk to them a month later about it.

When there are issues you need to address, it's important to bring them up in the right manner. You can say to a girl, "When I look at you time stands still" or you can say, "You have a face that would stop a clock." One of these gets the results you want and one gets you slapped. You can bring things out in a negative manner that creates push back or in a manner that makes progress.

6. Reinforcement

This is creating the motivating environment during the personal development interview by catching people doing things right.

Here's one example of how reinforcing properly works miracles.

When you're sitting down in an interview with someone, and you say, "Ben, tell me how you did that. You did a good job. Tell me how you did it." Ben wasn't watching himself do it. So, he gives you a combination, unconsciously, of what he perceived himself doing, and he kind of mingles it in with what he thinks you want to hear.

That's good. That is not bad. It's good because now the words come out of Ben's mouth. Ben's behavior begins to change in order to conform to the words that come out of his mouth. They bring what they should be doing up to a conscious level and walk out of the meeting saying, "That sounded pretty good. I think that's the way I'll do it."

That's the way behavior changes, and it changes in almost insignificant increments from week to week. You can't see it, but if you take a look from January to June, substantial behavior change takes place. The behavior change slows down if you do it every other week. The more behavior change you want, or the more opportunities to improve, the more often you conduct your PDIs.

7. Coaching

The manager has many roles. Sure you're a director, but you're also a leader, coach, counselor, motivator, trainer, administrator, and many more beyond that. In addition, whether you like it or not, the performance of individuals is often affected by domestic problems and you may need to help individuals get through them. We'll talk about this more under situational leadership.

This picture shows the wrong way to conduct a personal development interview.

This is the wrong way to conduct a personal development interview.

You don't want to sit on the other side of the desk when you conduct your PDIs. Sitting on the other side of the desk portrays authority. I'm the boss. You're the subordinate. Generally, the best way to hold the interview is by having the employee sit on the same side of the desk as you. You don't want to portray authority. You're a coach. You're a guide. You're a motivator. You want to help them grow and develop.

This is the right way to conduct a personal development interview.

You want to literally and figuratively be on the same side of the table working together.

Chapter 7

Situational Leadership Just Another "Feel-Good" Buzzword?

"To be honest, I know nothing about leading. But it's okay because my team knows nothing about following."

I'm mostly a black and white kind of guy. There's good, there's bad. There's right, there's wrong. There's proper behavior, there's stupid behavior. You succeed, or you fail; and you don't blame anyone else. So when I heard the term "Situational Leadership" I thought, *Holy cow, another feel-good, politically correct excuse for not performing.* I was wrong – way wrong.

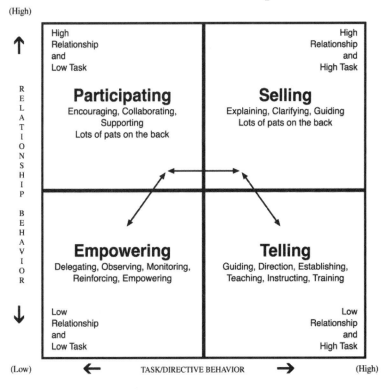

Situational Relationship Behavior is the extent to which the leader engages in 2-way communication; in other words, your interaction with people.

High relationship means you're highly engaged. You're giving them additional training and support on an ongoing basis. You're interacting with them quite frequently.

Low relationship behavior means that you're not as engaged in 2-way communication.

Task Behavior is the extent to which the leader is engaged in spelling out the duties and responsibilities. High task behavior means the manager is more detailed and directive toward telling the subordinate step-by-step what to do.

Low task behavior is when the manager assigns the task, delegates the task, and is not involved with actually getting the job done.

A new employee (team member) typically starts in Q1 and the manager does a lot of **Telling** (high task, low relationship). There is a lot of instruction showing them how to do the job. You're not patting them on the back yet because they haven't shown anything yet. You're teaching and training them, so there is not a lot of relationship behavior.

After a few months, the new employee is making some progress and it's time to move from telling to

Selling (high task, high relationship). The manager is still directing and showing, but the communication is more 2-way. The manager gives a lot of reinforcement while explaining, clarifying and persuading. The manager is mining for ideas from the team member and teaching them to think on their own. The leader still defines the roles and tasks, but seeks ideas and suggestions. The leader pats them on the back. The more you can guide them to thinking things out the more beneficial it is to you in the future.

As the individual grows, it's time for the manager to move from selling to **Participating** (high relationship, low task). The person understands the job and knows how to do it, but doesn't have a lot of confidence yet. They need reinforcement on an ongoing basis until they develop confidence. The manager gives the individual a lot of support, pats him on the back, and stays very close. Because the individual knows the job, there is much less directive behavior from the manager.

As the team member becomes more and more competent, he becomes a true expert at the job and the manager moves to **Empowering** (low relationship, low task). The team member is doing 80% or more of the talking during the PDI. The manager is observing, monitoring, reinforcing, and delegating.

Your goal as the manager is to get your staff to Quadrant 4, but as the graph above shows, it's not a one-way street. Depending on the job or task, you may move down or up a quadrant, or even two – and sometimes even three.

In one of my businesses, one of my vice presidents is fabulous at her job and my management style is almost always empowering. But she's not a numbers person, so when it comes to working with numbers my management style moves to Participating and sometimes to Selling or even Telling. With her it was not uncommon for me to say, "That number doesn't make sense, check it out."

It's also important to understand that you're working with people, not machines. We all have personal lives away from business and for all of us, **even us 5-percentors**, our personal lives influence us at work. Sometimes it's critically important to move down a quadrant when a team member has personal problems.

Leaving your empathy and understanding behind, you have a lot invested in someone who's in Q4. Moving up on the relationship scale to Participating or even to Selling is sometimes critical to get that person back up to speed. And, of course, if things get worse you may need to move to Telling.

Chapter 8

The Personal Development Interview… The Powering Force of an Effective Performance Management System

"My boss really screwed up today. He accidentally made me feel valued and respected."

Here are the five components you'll need for each position in your business in order to conduct effective personal development interviews:

Job Description
Objectives
Reportable Objectives
Activity Log
Interview Guide

We call these five components JORAIs. Some components of the JORAI are ever changing, and some are much more stagnant. Once you have a great Job Description it likely won't change much, but you'll certainly want to add, subtract, and edit it to some degree. The same goes for Objectives - you might add and subtract some, but not a lot.

Reportable Objectives, the Activity Log, and the Interview Guide should always be changing and evolving. As a reportable objective becomes routine for the person accomplishing it, you don't need to take time in your PDI to discuss it. It's time for that reportable objective to be relegated to an "Objective."

Here's an example of an objective that was reportable during PDI's, but is now relegated to an objective. This is in regards to providing Point-of-Sale computers to retailers. The reportable objective was, "Contact all new clients within two days after the arrival of the system and continue contacts on a systematic basis." That was an activity that was reported on during every PDI. We don't discuss this during our PDIs any longer because it is always accomplished. It has become routine. It is still included as an objective, but it is not a reportable objective that we discuss in PDIs.

Here's another example. A number of years ago we had an objective of shipping every order received by noon on the same day the order was received. FedEx comes every day at 4 P.M. We decided we wanted to do better, so we created this objective, "If the product is in stock, ship every order placed by 3:30 P.M. on the same day we receive the order." That became a reportable objective backed up by a time stamp on the order when it was entered, and a time stamp when it was shipped. We were able to track our progress towards the goal. After a while, meeting the goal was routine. We do it every day. That objective is still an objective. We don't want to lose sight of it. But it's not a reportable objective that gets discussed in a PDI.

Creating JORAIs

The best way to show you how to create and use JORAIs in your business is to give you an example.

Here is the JORAI for the sales manager of one of my businesses.

Job Description – The Job Description includes the job title, who the position reports to, what job positions report to this person, a summary of the position and the essential duties and responsibilities. To ensure that everyone knows what's expected, it is critical to have detailed duties and responsibilities. A great job description makes hiring the right person easier as well.

**American Retail Supply
Job Description**

Job Title: Vice President Sales
Reports to: President
Supervises: 10 Sales People, 1 Sales Assistant, 1 Receptionist, 1 Catalog Coordinator

SUMMARY
Responsible for the development of strategic goals and objectives for the American Retail Supply Sales Department. Also plans, organizes, coordinates and directs the activities of reporting personnel toward the achievement of such goals and objectives by performing the following duties personally or through subordinates.

ESSENTIAL DUTIES AND RESPONSIBILITIES include the following. Other duties may be assigned.
1. Participates with the President and other personnel in the development, implementation and updating of long term strategic and annual operational plans.
2. Develop the strategic goals and objectives for American Retail Supply Sales Department.
3. Oversee the achievement of the company's annual sales Objective.
4. Assign SMART (Specific, Measurable, Attainable, Relevant & Timed) objectives in areas of their job responsibilities for each of your direct reports.
5. Take the necessary action required to assure that all reports are on target to achieve their annual objectives or take the corrective action necessary to get them on target.
6. Establishes a man/woman power inventory by maintaining a continuous recruiting program for the strategic purpose of upgrading the caliber and productivity of employees in the sales organization.
7. Analyzes sales statistics to formulate policy and promote sales.

You get the idea. For our Vice President of Sales, the Job Description includes 31 more duties.

Objectives come directly from the Job Description. All objectives need to be S.M.A.R.T.

Specific - Objectives need to be specific. They need to be clear. Use exact numbers, dates, times, etc. State exactly what you want to accomplish. Who, what, where, and why.

Measurable – Objectives need to be measurable and big objectives need measurements along the way to achieving them. How will you demonstrate and evaluate the extent to which the objective has been accomplished?

Attainable - Objectives need to be realistic and attainable. While goals should stretch you and your team, they need to be realistic. It's often helpful to break a big objective into smaller objectives, so that you can continuously see progress that will keep you motivated to keep pushing forward.

Relevant – Objectives need to be relevant to the job description and getting the job done. The objective needs to tie into the key responsibilities of the job.

Timed – Objectives need to have a deadline, or timeframe for achieving your objective. Again, it's often helpful to break a big objective into smaller objectives with specific deadlines.

Here are the objectives for our Vice President of Sales. Notice, the first objective is to follow MJRs, identify deficiencies and correct the deficiencies.

Objectives
Vice President of Sales

- On an ongoing basis, maintain and write MJR's (Make You Happy Job Requirements) within the department. Use MAT's (Make You Happy Action Teams) as needed for development in areas of sales processes, satisfying client needs, reducing errors or eliminating future errors.
- On a continuous basis, maintain and update the company training manual. Train sales skills, product knowledge, and computer skills as it pertains to the sales department. Implement, participate and encourage those in the sales department in continual learning about the job, the industry, management, marketing, & sales techniques.
- On a regular preplanned basis, meet with each staff member within the sales department for scheduled PDI's (Personal Development Interviews) to increase skills, meet their goals and help motivate them to become the best they can be at their jobs.

- Weekly, Attend Personal Development Interviews with the CEO for the purpose of measuring progress toward objectives, reinforcement, and development. Collaborate on the sales department role, rules and overall direction.
- On a monthly basis, conduct routine sales meetings which are oriented around the three "I's" of meetings (Instructional, Informational, and Inspirational) that are pertinent to sales. Invite speakers, record meetings and distribute materials and recordings to other locations.
- On an ongoing basis, oversee and coordinate sample areas, showrooms, and tradeshows for the company. Develop processes for sending samples, trade show selling and showroom selling.
- On an ongoing basis, work with individual clients when called upon to help close sales, take care of specific client needs or in overflow situations.

The V.P. Sales has 27 more SMART objectives. A lot of these do not need to be reported upon as they have become routine.

Reportable Objectives - Our V.P. of Sales has 35 objectives. We can't possibly discuss all 35 objectives in our PDI's, so we need to narrow them down to 8-12 Reportable Objectives that we discuss in our weekly personal development interview.

Vice President Sales
20xx Reportable Objectives

1. On a weekly basis, take some specific and reportable action designed to increase the average annual sales per customer from $xxx.xx for the year 20xx to $xxx.xx for the year 20xx.
3. On a weekly basis throughout the year 20xx, take some specific and reportable action designed to increase market share from xx,xxx customers to xx,xxx.
4. On a weekly basis, take some specific and reportable action designed to increase the average order from $xxx.xx for the year 20xx to $xxx.xx for the year 20xx.
6. On a preplanned basis, conduct PDI's (Personal Development Interviews) with each of the reporting sales personnel for the purpose of measuring progress against objectives, taking corrective action, increasing skills, and helping them motivate themselves to become the best they can be at their jobs.
7. On a preplanned basis, attend a Personal Development Interview with the CEO for the purpose of measuring progress toward objectives, reinforcement, and development.
8. On a weekly basis, take some specific and reportable action to create a motivating environment throughout the company by catching people doing things right and reinforcing them for such actions.
9. On a monthly basis, with a focus towards achieving the company sales objective for 20xx, take specific and reportable action to assure that all reports are on target

for achieving their annual objectives or take the corrective action necessary to get them on target.
10. On a weekly basis find something that is broken and fix it.

Activity Log – Between each PDI, the individual being interviewed records the activities he has taken in each area on his activity log. Notice, the activity log emphasizes action and activity. **There should be enough room after each question for the interviewee to make notes for the activities.**

You want to be sure that every PDI starts on a positive note, so start each PDI with the question, "What went right since we last met?" This question is included on the Activity Log so the individual has time to think about it and report on something positive.

Even with this, sometimes the individual will say, "Nothing went right." It is your job to turn this around, and make it a positive, or at a minimum, a learning experience. Your response to, "Nothing went right" should be, "Tell me what went wrong?"

After the individual answers, "What went wrong?" you then ask, "What did you learn from that?" You then need to make sure that this leads to learning something positive.

It's important that your managers understand that they often are not responsible for doing these activities, but are responsible for coaching their team so they are done.

Here's an example from the activity log below. Our VP of Sales has a reportable objective of, "On a weekly basis, take some specific and reportable action designed to increase the average annual sales per customer from $xxx.xx for the year 20xx to $xxx.xx for the year 20xx."

She can "do" things that lead to achieving that goal, or she can coach team members to do things to achieve the goal.

She could "do" something by creating a campaign that the sales reps could use to sell higher priced items, or research the addition of products to our product line.

Or she could report on what she did to coach a team member to achieve the goal. She could report that she identified that Jane is not making progress on increasing the average annual sales per customer, and what Jane and her are doing to correct the action.

Or she might report that Fred is doing a great job increasing the average annual sales per customer because he's concentrating on mentioning add on items on each call and we've shared this with the rest of the team.

It's important for the manager to understand that they're not just reporting on what they do, but on what they do to coach their team.

Here is the Activity Log for our Vice President of Sales.

Vice President Sales
20xx Activity Log

1. What went right this week?
2. Report on sales objectives. Written and Shipped – Last 5 days, MTD, last 30 days and year-to-date.
3. Action taken to increase the average annual sales per customer from $xxx.xx for the year 20xx to $xxx.xx for the year 20xx.
4. Action taken to increase market share from xx,xxx customers to xx,xxx.
5. Action taken to increase the average order from $xxx.xx for the year 20xx to $xxx.xx for the year 20xx.
6. Action taken to conduct PDIs (Personal Development Interviews) with each of the reporting sales personnel for the purpose of measuring progress against objectives, taking corrective action, increasing skills, and helping them motivate themselves to become the best they can be at their jobs
7. Action taken to attend a Personal Development Interview with the CEO for the purpose of measuring

progress toward objectives, reinforcement, and development.
8. Action taken to create a motivating environment throughout the company by catching people doing things right and reinforcing them for such actions.
9. Action taken to assure that all reports are on target for achieving their annual objectives or take the corrective action necessary to get them on target.
10. Action take to find something that is broken and fix it.
11. Actions not shown above.

Interview Guide - The interview guide is used by the manager as their guide for the interview. To create the interview guide, simply turn reportable objectives into questions. Be sure to add the questions, "What action did you take that we didn't talk about?" and "Is there anything else you want to talk about?" at the end of every interview.

You should leave enough room to write notes between each question. Writing notes shows the interviewee that you're paying attention. It will also create some natural quiet time in which the interviewee will add to his responses, and that's good. Writing notes will also help you with your summary at the end of your Personal Development Interview. The good summary is critical to getting the interviewee to leave the interview pumped up and ready to take on the world.

Suggestion – Write your notes in black or blue ink. If you ask a question that requires a follow up by either you or the interviewee, circle your note with a red pen and make sure you address these after the PDI, or during the next PDI.

As we discussed earlier, PDIs should be very positive experiences for both the manager and the interviewee. This is where you catch people doing things right, reinforce that behavior, and create a positive growing business.

**Vice President Sales
2011 Interview Guide**

1. What went right this week?
2. How did we do on our sales objectives since we last met? Written and Shipped – Last 5 days, MTF, last 30 days, year-to-date.
3. What action did you, or your reports take to increase the average annual sales per customer from $x,xxx for the year 20xx to $x,xxx for the year 20xx?
4. What action did you, or your reports, take to increase the market share from xx,xxx customers to xx,xxx?

5. What action did you, or your reports, take to increase the average order from $xxx for the year 20xx to $xxx for the year 20xx.
6. What action did you take to conduct PDIs (Personal Development Interviews) with each of the reporting sales personnel for the purpose of measuring progress against objectives, taking corrective action, increasing skills, and helping them motivate themselves to become the best they can be at their jobs?
7. What action did you take to attend a Personal Development Interview with the CEO for the purpose of measuring progress toward objectives, reinforce, and development?
8. What action did you take to create a motivating environment throughout the company by catching people doing things right and reinforcing them for such actions.
9. What action did you take to assure that all reports are on target for achieving their annual objective, or what action did you take to get them on target?
10. What action did you take to find something that is broken and fix it.?
11. What actions did you take that are not shown above?
12. Is there anything else you would like to discuss?

PDI Summary: One of the best parts of your PDI is the summary. Use the notes you've taken to summarize what has been accomplished. This is incredibly motivating for both the interviewer and the interviewee. You'll summarize what's been discussed in the interview and every time the manager and the interviewee leave pumped up and ready to take on the world.

Chapter 9

Putting It All Together

"We interrupt sounds of the ocean for this special news bulletin: Back at the office, everyone is getting along just fine without you!"

I met Vince Zirpoli in 2005. By that time, I had been running American Retail Supply for 24 years. Our customer service was top notch, we had excellent products, sales people, staff, and marketing; and we had systemized everything in the business so it was running very well. We took care of clients well, and our system insured that we made very few mistakes. But I knew our performance management sucked.

Over the years we had tried performance reviews and found they sucked and were actually counterproductive so we stopped them. We replaced them with just trying to stay in touch. Then we thought we found a better way to do performance reviews so we tried them again – found they still sucked, stopped again – rinse and repeat.

When I listened to Vince I knew I found the answer.

I hired Vince to help me put together our Performance Management System, paid him tens of thousands of dollars and it turned out to be one of the best investments I've ever made.

We now not only had top notch customer service, fabulous products, superb sales people and staff, great marketing and systems to ensure we did things right, we now were getting the very best out of every team member, getting total buy-in from them in achieving our goals, and getting great ideas to improve the business from every team member.

As the owner of the business I had made it to the place that we're all looking for – freedom. The team was functioning so well that I was free to spend my time on the really important things in my business. Free to work where I wanted – from the lake house in Washington, the river house in Montana, or sitting on the beach in Hawaii.

Financially free. Free to start other businesses including Keith Lee Business System which is dedicated to "Teaching business owners how to create highly productive teams so they can control their business and their life and finally be free."

As I write this in 2015, Vince Zirpoli is 87 years old.

As you can see, Vince looks a lot like Brad Pitt.
I had to put that in, Vince loves saying that.

Knowing that Vince wants his Performance Management System to live beyond his time, I approached him to get the rights to use what he taught me and all of his archives to create the Make-You-Happy Performance Management System with the goal of creating a Performance Management System that business owners like you can implement in your business for a tiny fraction of what I paid to get it going in my business. Vince was thrilled to hear about my plans and gladly sold me the rights.

I mentioned the financial freedom that comes from owning a well-run business that gets the best out of every team member, gets buy-in from everyone, and gets everyone involved daily with improvement. With that, in 2015, I sold American Retail Supply and am financially secure for life. That's what I want to create for you, life-time financial security and freedom. Vince loved one-on-one consulting, and so do I. But my dream is to get my system into the hands of tens of thousands of business owners and change the lives of a million people.

I know that when I help ten thousand business owners have better businesses they will be better parents, spouses, employers, friends, relatives, and business associates. And I know that when team members (employees) understand that they are important, that their ideas are important, that they make a difference they will go home and be better parents, spouses, employers, friends, relatives. And then all of these people will affect the lives of everyone around them. I know, that sounds kind of touchy feely, but it is my dream.

With that, I'm thrilled to let you know about the Make-You-Happy Performance Management System, the system that makes you happy, your team members happy, your customers happy, and yes even your spouse and kids happy.

As I mentioned, Vince spent decades helping more than one hundred businesses create the training and JORAIs they needed to implement his Performance Management featuring Personal Development Interviews in their businesses. His archives of training material and JORAIs created for hundreds of positions are enormous. In addition, Vince recorded 4-1/2 hours of video training on his system.

When I got everything I was blown away. I call it Vince's Treasure Chest.

We spent hundreds of hours going through everything I got from Vince, and then creating a fill in the blanks, step-by-step program that you can implement yourself, to get everyone in your business working together and functioning as a highly productive team, and give you the freedom you've always hoped for.

Here's how you'll do it.

First you'll listen to the Fast Start CD that walks you through everything. You'll quickly see that this is an easy to implement step-by-step system.

You'll then lock your door, get a refreshment, and watch the three DVDs - each with 1-1/2 hours of training from Vince. Along with the DVDs you'll get a transcript of the DVDs so you can highlight what you want.

While watching these, you'll discover everything you need to know to get up and going and to start creating highly productive teams. You'll discover why you need a performance management system (I know, you already know, but you'll use these same DVDs to teach your managers.), and how to eliminate demotivating and counter-productive Performance Reviews and replace them with motivating, inspirational, and most importantly; **productive** Personal Development Interviews that get the performance you want.

You'll discover how to turn negatives into positives, how to get every team member to subconsciously learn how to do their job better than they thought they could. You'll discover how to get every person excited about doing a good job and contributing to improvement.

You'll now go through the rest of the materials you've received in the program and follow the step-by-step instructions. You're now ready to show it to your managers'.

Have each of them read this little book. Then schedule three - 2 hour meetings with your managers. In these meetings, you'll watch the four and a half hours of training from Vince and discuss it with your team.

Pick one manager to work with. Pick someone who is excited about getting the best out of everyone on their team. The first thing you'll do is create a JORAI for this manager. But again, don't worry, your manager will actually create their JORAI for their position and they'll use templates to get it done quickly and easily. Remember a JORAI is:

- Job Description
- Objectives
- Reportable Objectives
- Activity Log
- Interview Guide

Your manager will get the templates so he can create his JORAI quickly and easily using Vince's Treasure Chest.

I don't believe in recreating the wheel. Why should you start something from scratch when you can easily use something that already exists and just tweak it to work for you?

The program includes job descriptions for each of the follow management positions:

VP Operations	VP Information Systems
VP Sales	VP Marketing
Regional Manager	Purchasing Manager
Branch Manager	Warehouse Manager
Closing Manager	Call Center Manager
Controller	Finishing Service Manager
Deputy Director	Design Center Manager
Design Manager	Client Service Manager
Pre-Press Manager	Loan Servicing Manager
Plant Manager	Flower Processing Manager
Shop Manager	Department Manager
Wedding Manager	Underwriting Manager
Satellite Supervisor	Accounting Manager

Mortgage Operations Manager
Computer Systems Coordinator
Technology Manager

Each of these job descriptions were written by the master himself, Vince Zirpoli, or me.

All you need to do is ask your manager to look at a job title that is somewhat similar to theirs and tweak it to work for them. They can of course look at a few others also, but they will undoubtedly be able to create a job description that works for them in no time.

From there it's easy for the manager, using the example in the program to create objectives, reportable objectives, activity log and interview guide for their position. It is a simple step-by-step process to follow.

Now it's time to move on to the Personal Development Interview (PDI). Vince talks extensively about PDIs in the DVDs and I includ several samples of actual PDIs to get you up to speed. In addition, the program includes evaluation forms so you can evaluate your PDIs and those of your managers' to continually improve.

You get eight audio CDs of actual PDIs and an evaluation of each. Five of these PDIs are me interviewing my managers, and three are of managers' interviewing their reports.

You'll listen to each of these, review the evaluation, and discover how to do them yourself.

Now, it's time for your PDI with your manager. The manager will fill out his activity log for the week and then you'll conduct your PDI. Record the PDI. You'll evaluate the PDI and ask the manager you interviewed to evaluate it also. You are already to the half way point to creating highly productive teams, controlling your business and your life, and freedom!

For the next few weeks you and your manager conduct your PDIs, evaluate each one, and improve each week. Once you're somewhat comfortable it's time for you to get your other managers on board and time for your manager to get his subordinates (reports) on board.

You simply rinse and repeat what you did with the first manager with the rest of your managers and have your managers do the same with their reports.

The system includes the JORAIs that Vince used to create PDIs for 254 different job descriptions. Your manager's will undoubtedly be able to find positions that are similar and use them as the model they need.

To get the Make-You-Happy Performance Management System powered by Personal Development Interviews go to www.KeithLee.com/pdi. Discover how to create highly productive teams, control your business and your life, and be truly FREE.